Intentional Love

A 21-Day Interactive Guide
to Intentionally Transform Your Marriages

By

Greg & Shonda Holmes

Intentional Love

A 21-Day Interactive Guide
to Intentionally Transform Your Marriages

*And be not conformed to this world: but be
ye transformed by the renewing of your
mind, that ye may prove what is that good,
and acceptable, and perfect, will of God.*
Romans 12:2

Dedication

Special thanks to God Almighty and our Lord Jesus Christ for your love, grace and mercy to us. We are grateful and we know that it is with your power and strength that our marriage has been blessed to thrive.

We dedicate this book to the loving memory of our precious babies, Gregorie and Jordan Holmes. Gregorie, your dream came true. You always said daddy and mommy would do ministry together. We will forever love and miss you both.

Acknowledgements

Special thanks to:

To our parents Mr. & Mrs. LJ Flowers and Mrs. Beulah Holmes Albritton and her husband Mr. Johnny Albritton, we love you all. We appreciate you for the love and the Godly examples that you have been before us.

To the loving memory of Pop, Harry Glenn Holmes, Sr., we love you dearly. We miss you and we are thankful for your countless words of wisdom.

To our darling daughters Jaala, Zuri, Madison Holmes and our sweetheart Camille (Desmond) Primo. All of you have a special place in our hearts, we love you dearly. We know that we haven't been perfect, but we hope that our marriage has been one that you can use as a model for your marriages.

To our siblings Harry G. (Pam) Holmes Jr., Sherida Holmes, John Holmes, Pete (Myra) Moore, Rhonda (Darryll) Corpening and Mark (Tina) Flowers, thanks for sharing your lives and experiences with us. We appreciate your prayers and your support. A special thanks to our dearest friends Gina & Charles Bracks.

To the WHO & WOO, our friends and power couples, your continued push and prayers kept us encouraged throughout this process to complete our book. We are grateful to call you our brothers and sisters. Thank you *WOOWHO* we love you!

FOREWORD

It is our pleasure to be writing this foreword for our dear brother and sister, Elders Greg and Shonda Holmes. Most times a book is recommended for content only, however we are endorsing both the writers and what they have written. We refer to Greg and Shonda, as the "power couple." Their marriage of over thirty years has weathered the seasons of youthful love and sex to mature respect and loving commitment. They know what it means to persevere, to overcome tragedy, and to rise above their circumstances. They are anointed by God to share spiritual principles, the triumphs and the tragedies of covenant marriage, and the blessings that come from a marriage submitted to God.

Greg and Shonda have been a safe haven for many couples who were ready to throw in the towel. They are well equipped to minister healing, facilitate deliverance, and encourage restoration. There is life after an affair, life after financial destruction, and life after heart breaking sicknesses and situations that have the potential to negatively impact, weaken, and destroy marriages.

21 Days to Intentional Love is an interactive journal that will provide you with more than just philosophical thoughts; it is anointed to empower couples in their quest to have a marriage that exemplifies Christ and the Church.

Focused on an Eternal Legacy,
Drs. Ben and Sherry Gaither
Stronghold Christian Church

Contents

Introduction

God is INTENTIONAL about LOVE! He created the institution of marriage and He declared it good. God's intent for the honorable union of marriage was for two to become one in a loving relationship. In Genesis 2:24 scripture shares, "Therefore shall a man leave his father and his mother and shall cleave unto his wife and they shall be one flesh." The beauty of love is expressed in the oneness of marriage when two people are willing to cherish each other regardless of their differences. Each couple must build their relationship on love and trust with a plan to work together in the good times and when trouble is present. For many marriages the honeymoon is over and the lingering question is what do we do next? In this writing, you will find that your next is now. Marriages are under attack simply because God deemed the union honorable. The enemy does not want to see marriages succeed, so he attacks marriages in many ways. We have selected twenty-one topics that marriages struggle with daily and some of the obstacles that our marriage faced in becoming unified.

We pray that if you are reading our book, Intentional Love, that you will be blessed and grow in your marriage. Use this interactive guide to learn how to build intentional love and make the commitment to eliminate bad habits.

It is our hope that in the next twenty-one days your marriage will flourish. Prayerfully you will both be overcome with intentional love that will cause your relationship to soar to heights unknown. We encourage you to read each day and complete the exercises with sincerity. Decree and declare the blessing of the Lord over your marriage. Write your daily outcome to note your progress and to see how your relationship has grown. After you have completed the entire book, sit down together and observe where you started, the attacks and blessings along the way and your final outcome.

For the spouse that chooses to purchase and read our book alone, stand still and don't give up. Hold on to the hope of intentional love for your marriage. Our prayers are with you. Trust God to make the difference. We may not know your name, but we are praying for your freedom in your marriage and the unity you deserve.

Remember, reading and having a desire alone won't bring the change you need. To enjoy intentional love, you must do the work daily even beyond the twenty-one days.

Use this 21-Day Interactive Guide Daily to:
1. Read the **Topic Daily** that you need.
2. Make a **Daily Declaration**
3. Honor the **Daily Intent.**
4. Track your **Daily Outcome**.
5. Memorize the **Daily Intentional Tools.**
6. Write your prayer and **Pray Daily**.
7. **Initial** your commitment **Daily**.

Remember, little steps create big changes.

Day 1

Intentionally Loving

Love suffers long *and* is kind; love does not envy; love does not parade itself, is not puffed up; does not behave rudely, does not seek its own, is not provoked, thinks no evil; does not rejoice in iniquity, but rejoices in the truth; bears all things, believes all things, hopes all things, endures all things. I Corinthians 13:4 - 7

He said, "who loves you baby?" I said, "I love you!"

In our own way, each of us expressed our true love to one another. We had an overwhelming rush of emotions and a desire to be together forever. Neither one of us wanted those days to end. Within the first year, I got pregnant and we had a son. He was so precious and his presence filled our hearts with joy. As the years went by, we learned that even the best marriages experience conflict. Our love was challenged as we tried to learn how to grow together. Some days our communication reflected a beautiful ray of sunshine and then there were those days that it reflected a wind storm. My husband never wanted to talk about our issues and I was determined to talk about them all.

Once reality set in and the wave of emotional sunshine subsided, neither the question of love nor the confirming response, was enough to keep our smile. We got stuck. Was it really love? Was our love enough?

Our love was intentional but it wasn't enough to keep us from heartache and crisis. Both of us had unrealistic expectations and neither of us knew how to fix what was broken. We needed the Lord in our relationship. We realized that without God in our hearts, it would be impossible to love by His design.

Was it really love? Yes! Was our love enough? Yes! We know now what we didn't know then, and we are intentionally loving this life together. Our strong desire and intent to stay in love helped us to remember that in our own strength we could never overcome our issues. Learning to disagree peacefully and keep our dignity was a great lesson, a lesson that continues. We intentionally turned our individual desires and concerns over to God. With His love we began learning how to love on purpose and unconditionally. True love is worth fighting for together!

Intentionally Declare

I declare and decree that our love will survive through test
and trials. I declare we will live faithfully and lovingly
together in the Name of Jesus. I will put God first in my
marriage and my relationship with my spouse.

Declare:

_____

_____

_____

_____

_____

Think about the issues that you are facing in your marriage that make it hard to intentionally love each another.

*******DAILY INTENT*******

Write one thing you will intentionally do today to show your love to your spouse that may have been an issue for you before.

_____

_____

_____

Outcome:

_____

_____

_____

Intentional Tools

For I have come to have much joy and comfort in your love…

Philemon 7:1

We love him, because he first loved us.

1 John 4:19

Beloved, let us love one another: for love is of God; and every one that loves is born of God, and knows God.

1 John 4:7

If ye love me, keep my commandments.

John 14:15

There is no fear in love; but perfect love cast out fear: because fear hath torment. He that fears is not made perfect in love.

1 John 4:18

His Initials   Date   Her Initials   Date

Commit to Daily Prayer

Use today's topic and write a prayer for your spouse.
Earnestly commit to pray for them daily.

_____

_____

_____

_____

_____

Day 2

Intentionally Thoughtful

Finally, brethren, whatsoever things are true, whatsoever things are honest, whatsoever things are just, whatsoever things are pure, whatsoever things are lovely, whatsoever things are of good report; if there be any virtue, and if there be any praise, think on these things. Philippians 4:8

The art of being thoughtful is precious. Genuine thoughtfulness expresses to your spouse that you honor them as you make decisions that impact them. There is nothing more frustrating than for a husband or wife to feel left out or ignored. Many times our ignorance of how our spouse may feel about a situation will create unnecessary tension, because our actions appear selfish. Thoughtless behavior may seem insignificant to the person doing it, but to the one on the receiving end it is very unpleasant. Intentionally consider your spouse daily.

If both the husband and the wife would recognize that thoughtfulness benefits both the giver and the receiver, consideration would be viewed as a gift. Ask their opinion about things, remember their response for the next time, don't trivialize their desires and be thoughtful even when it hurts. Thoughtlessness can easily be coupled with selfishness and bring chaos into your home.

Be careful not to be rude and uncaring to your spouse. Teach each other how you want to be treated. Follow the golden rule and show the same thoughtfulness to your spouse that you desire and deserve. Be mindful that you are not more thoughtful at church, work or with extended family than you are with your spouse. If either spouse notices a rise in this type of behavior, ask questions. Ask in a loving and thoughtful manner, with a sincere desire to fix the problem. Be open to hear and slow to speak. Refrain from using negative words. Remain thoughtful.

Greg likes to watch football and I like to watch Lifetime movies. We usually spend time together before the games during football season. While he is comfortable in his man cave watching the game, I am enjoying a great Lifetime movie with our girls. We entertain each other with what is important to us. This level of respect and thoughtfulness keeps peace in the home. Remember, even the small things count.

Intentionally Declare

I come against all negative thoughts, actions, and words that were spoken over my marriage. I declare peace where there is strife whether it was caused by me or another in the Name of Jesus. I will put God first in my marriage and my relationship with my spouse.

Declare:

_____

_____

_____

_____

_____

Think of the most recent time that you were thoughtful to your spouse. Would he/she agree? Y__ N__

List three ways you are willing to intentionally show thoughtful behavior to your spouse today.

1._____
2._____
3._____

Outcome:

_____

_____

_____

Intentional Tools

For his merciful kindness is great toward us: and the truth of the LORD endureth forever. Praise ye the LORD.

Psalms 117:2

O that they were wise, that they understood this that they would consider their latter end!

Deuteronomy 32:29

Only fear the LORD, and serve him in truth with all your heart: for consider how great things he hath done for you.

I Samuel 12:24

Put on therefore, as the elect of God, holy and beloved, bowels of mercies, kindness, humbleness of mind, meekness, longsuffering;

Colossians 3:12

His Initials   Date   Her Initials   Date

Commit to Daily Prayer

Use today's topic and write a prayer for your spouse.
Earnestly commit to pray for them daily.

_____

_____

_____

_____

_____

Day 3

Intentionally Delivered

I sought the Lord and He heard me and delivered me from
all my fears. Psalms 34:4

Trigger words. Have you ever been called out of your
name? Has anyone ever teased you and negatively used
adjectives to describe you?

Words such as, sensitive, stupid, emotional, strange,
slow, or lazy, can be damaging. Sometimes, the words that
were said to us and about us as a child lingered in our
minds and caused deep wounds.

Now as adults many of us are still wounded and we find
ourselves trapped in that emotional space for years without
deliverance. We may have been seven years old or
otherwise at the time of the offense and emotionally the
hurt never healed. Gripped by the torment of those words
we find ourselves paralyzed and subject to anger, rejection,
anxiety and sometimes pity.

Many of us are good executives, pastors, preachers,
leaders, administrators, parents, managers and such, but

emotionally we are undelivered. Even as Christians, things that we won't completely deal with, will deal with us.

Our spouses are usually closer to us than anyone else and sometimes we find it painful to share our deepest concerns. The thought of being criticized or minimized again creates fear and causes us to shut down. Not only are we in bondage, but we are holding our spouses in bondage and often for a wound perhaps they didn't cause.

Don't allow the events of your past to keep you from enjoying a healthy life and marriage. Fight fear with faith and trust God to deliver you and everything attached to you. Forgive your offenders and live in wholeness and holiness. God calls us the "apple of His eye!" Believe it, we are special to Him. As you seek God for deliverance, totally surrender your fear and your pain. Trust God and He will deliver you from all of your fears. Remember, when God speaks of His children He uses words such as, "BELOVED," "BLESSED," "PRECIOUS," "ANOINTED," "SON," and "DAUGHTER!"

Intentionally Declare

I declare and decree every ungodly voice that has been spoken over my marriage be silenced now in the Name of Jesus. I will put God first in my marriage and my relationship with my spouse.

Declare:

_____

_____

_____

_____

_____

Make a decision to share your deepest hurt with your spouse today.

*******DAILY INTENT*******

Intentionally write down the words from your past that have caused you pain and ask your spouse to pray with you as you forgive and release your offender.

Write a letter to your spouse asking them to forgive you for holding them as your offender and thank them for their support.

_____

_____

_____

Outcome:

_____

_____

_____

Intentional Tools

Confess your faults one to another, and pray one for another, that ye may be healed. The effectual fervent prayer of a righteous man availeth much.

James 5:16

Be pleased, O LORD, to deliver me: O LORD, make haste to help me.

Psalms 40:13

The Lord knoweth how to deliver the godly out of temptations, and to reserve the unjust unto the day of judgment to be punished:

II Peter 2:9

Stand fast therefore in the liberty wherewith Christ hath made us free, and be not entangled again with the yoke of bondage.

Galatians 5:1

His Initials   Date   Her Initials   Date

Commit to Daily Prayer

Use today's topic and write a prayer for your spouse.
Earnestly commit to pray for them daily.

_____

_____

_____

_____

_____

Day 4

Intentionally Peaceful

And let the peace of God rule in your hearts, to the which also ye are called in one body; and be ye thankful. Colossians 3:15

One of the most important things in life is peace. God has promised to give us the peace that surpasses all understanding (Phil. 4:7).

In our fast paced society, we tend to treat life as a sprint instead of the marathon that takes us at a slower pace. We overload our schedules and live under an unbalanced load of pressure that wears our patience. We fail to realize that overindulgence drains us and causes us to be short tempered and unpleasant to those around us.

Many of us were raised in families where there was not much peace. We learned and developed unhealthy attitudes about the simple things of life. Some households spoke in very loud tones to one another and aired their differences while other households kept their anger to themselves. Neither choice promotes peace and harmony, especially when there is no resolve. We must decide to speak well to and of one another in peace. Every aspect of our lives will be adversely affected when our peace is broken. Proverbs 15:13 encourages us to have a cheerful countenance.

I admonish husbands and wives to make a conscious decision to walk in peace together. Pray for one another. Ask God for a heart that will be obedient to Him. Intentionally pray for peace, a spirit of praise, humility, love and thanksgiving. Then wait on God to manifest the change you have prayed about. Praise Him in advance for a life of peace that is God controlled, rather than a life of chaos that is controlled by your flesh.

One of my favorite scriptures that my grandmother taught me as a young woman dealt with the peace of God. Numbers 6:24-26, "The Lord bless you and keep you; the Lord make his face to shine upon you, and be gracious unto you; the Lord lift up His countenance upon you, and give you peace."

Intentionally Declare

I declare and decree the peace of God that surpasses all understanding will be upon my marriage in the Name of Jesus. I will put God first in my marriage and my relationship with my spouse.

Declare:

_____

_____

_____

_____

_____

Think of the unhealthy ways that you have broken the peace in your relationship.

******* *DAILY INTENT*******

Identify the things your spouse says or does that often disturbs your peace. Ask yourself why these actions provoke the given response from you.

Write a plan of how you will possess your thoughts when you feel you are about to lose control.

_____

_____

_____

Outcome:

_____

_____

_____

Intentional Tools

Blessed are the peacemakers: for they shall be called the children of God.

Matthew 5:9

Peace I leave with you, my peace I give unto you: not as the world giveth, give I unto you. Let not your heart be troubled, neither let it be afraid.

John 14:27

For he that will love life, and see good days, let him refrain his tongue from evil, and his lips that they speak no guile: Let him eschew evil, and do good; let him seek peace, and ensue it.

I Peter 3:10 & 11

Now no chastening for the present seemeth to be joyous, but grievous: nevertheless afterward it yieldeth the peaceable fruit of righteousness unto them which are exercised thereby.

Hebrews 12:11

His Initials   Date   Her Initials   Date

Commit to Daily Prayer

Use today's topic and write a prayer for your spouse.
Earnestly commit to pray for them daily.

_____

_____

_____

_____

_____

Day 5
Intentionally Forgive

Then came Peter to him, and said, Lord, how oft shall my
brother sin against me, and I forgive him? Till seven times?
Jesus saith unto him, I say not unto thee, until seven times:
but, until seventy times seven. Matthew 18:21-22

Relax. I hear you saying, I am tired and I have run out
of grace to forgive again. It isn't fair, it isn't right! God
please fix this and reveal that it isn't my fault and that I
have done all that I need to do. It sounds like you are
keeping a score card on who's right or wrong and how
many times you have forgiven your offender. Look at the
scripture above and notice the word UNTIL. God didn't
leave it up to us to decide when we should stop forgiving
those that hurt us. God said UNTIL. You're right, I wasn't
present and neither do I know how painful your story is to
you, but God is well aware. FORGIVE your spouse and
ask God to help you love them as He loves them. Release
your spouse and watch God release you.

The Color Purple is one of my favorite movies. I have
memorized and can recite many of the lines from several of
the actors. This movie came out in the 80's and over

twenty years later my memory bank still holds the scenes. Just like a good movie, we have a habit of rewinding our thoughts and replaying them over and over again in our minds. Sometimes we press the record button and every hurt and pain is recorded to watch later. Real talk, some movies need to be deleted from the play list in our minds. Press delete and not replay. Reconnect to the spirit of the Lord and allow him to minister His love and peace to your soul. Don't allow your thoughts or your offender to hold you captive with negative thoughts or memories. Look within and ask God to heal your heart. Ask God to restore you and lead you as you walk through this period of forgiveness. Speak the word of God over your life and shut down the voice of the enemy that comes to convince you that you are entitled to continue to walk in your flesh and feel like you feel.

Remember, when you ask God to forgive your sins, He will, and He expects you to forgive others. God holds each of us responsible for ourselves and He desires to bless us for our obedience to Him. Be intentional, forgive and be forgiven!

Intentionally Declare

I decree that the pain of unforgiveness, jealousy, bitterness, anger, hurt, a lying tongue, and every evil act will no longer hold my marriage in bondage. I declare total freedom and forgiveness in my marriage in the Name of Jesus. I will put God first in my marriage and my relationship with my spouse.

Declare:

_____

_____

_____

_____

_____

_____

Are you willing to press DELETE on past negativity and stop REPLAYING those events?

*******DAILY INTENT*******

Intentionally write down the negative scenes from your past that need to be replaced with positive scenes. Ask God to heal your heart and allow you to forgive and walk daily in the power of forgiveness.

Stand face to face with your spouse and ask them to forgive you and tell them that you forgive them. Ask your spouse to share with you what offended them. Stay calm.

_____

_____

_____

Outcome:

_____

_____

_____

Intentional Tools

He that covereth a transgression seeketh love; but he that repeateth a matter separateth very friends.

Proverbs 17:9

For if ye forgive men their trespasses, your heavenly Father will also forgive you.

Matthew 6:14

And be ye kind one to another, tenderhearted, forgiving one another, even as God for Christ's sake hath forgiven you.

Ephesians 4:32

For thou, Lord, art good, and ready to forgive; and plenteous in mercy unto all them that call upon thee.

Psalms 86:5

His Initials   Date   Her Initials   Date

Commit to Daily Prayer

Use today's topic and write a prayer for your spouse.
Earnestly commit to pray for them daily.

_____

_____

_____

_____

_____

Day 6

Intentionally Agree

Can two walk together, unless they agree? Amos 3:3

In June 1987, Greg and I said I do. We committed to live and love as one without knowing how our decisions would impact our lives. Thirty years later, we can both say that we are still bringing our desires to the table and working through them together. It hasn't always been easy to agree on everything, but we have never stopped trying. Some of what we have experienced has been very painful, but we have endured it together. In some areas, one of us may have been a little more passionate about a particular desire than the other but we supported each other's decision or we didn't do it. Faith and finances have a way of tearing even the strongest marriages apart, but God has been faithful to us.

We moved to Georgia from Texas over 20 years ago. Greg was in the middle of a shift in his career and he wanted to leave Dallas and relocate to Norcross. Initially, I didn't agree with the move because my career was going well and financially we were not in danger. As the head of our family, Greg made the decision to relocate and as difficult as it was for me to agree, I packed my bags. I prayed and I cried because I didn't want to move. I asked God to fix my heart and touch my mouth and keep me from saying everything that I was thinking. I also asked God to direct our paths and to make our way prosperous. God was faithful to us. Our commitment to God and one another grew stronger each day and we refused to allow this major shift to destroy our lives. We downsized our lives but not our love. We sold our home in Texas and moved into a duplex in Georgia.

Living in Texas, we were away from our family and we spent a lot of money several times a year flying home to visit. This move to Georgia brought us closer to home. We had family living in the city and the rest of our family was within a 4 to 6 hour drive away.

I loved living in Dallas, I loved our new home and I loved my job! More importantly, I love my husband and living in the will of God. It takes a lot of energy and hurtful emotions to disagree but great joy comes with seeking God for His will and walking it out in peace. Two can only walk together if they agree.

Intentionally Declare

I declare and decree every ungodly voice that has been spoken over my marriage be silenced now in the Name of Jesus. I will put God first in my marriage and my relationship with my spouse.

Declare:

_____

_____

_____

_____

_____

Are you and your spouse walking as one?

Intentionally write down the things that you disagree on and agree to pray over them for the next seven days.

Next, revisit the list and discuss your thoughts respectfully.

_____

_____

_____

Outcome:

_____

_____

_____

Intentional Tools

Fulfil ye my joy, that ye be likeminded, having the same love, being of one accord, of one mind.

Philippians 2:2

Finally, be ye all of one mind, having compassion one of another, love as brethren, be pitiful, be courteous.

I Peter 3:8

Now I beseech you, brethren, by the name of our Lord Jesus Christ, that ye all speak the same thing, and [that] there be no divisions among you; but [that] ye be perfectly joined together in the same mind and in the same judgment.

I Corinthians 1:10

And above all these things put on charity, which is the bond of perfectness.

Colossians 3:14

His Initials   Date   Her Initials   Date

Commit to Daily Prayer

Use today's topic and write a prayer for your spouse.
Earnestly commit to pray for them daily.

_____

_____

_____

_____

_____

Day 7

Intentionally Worship

And at midnight Paul and Silas prayed and sang praises
unto God, and the prisoners heard them. Acts 16:25

Like Paul and Silas, we must worship God together,
even when we don't know how He is going to work it out.

Worship includes prayer, praise and devotion. When
you became one in marriage, God gave you a lifetime
partner in worship. Beware of the situations that pull your
marriage away from worship. Don't leave God out of your
marriage and begin to worship each other instead of Him.
Don't allow the love of God to be dampened by the frills of
life that create sadness and turn you away from Him and
away from one another. Call a timeout from disagreements
to get in the face of God together. Stop the bleeding and
begin interceding. Use your weapons of warfare to work
for you instead of against you. We can make a habit out of
anything that we desire. Get in the habit of quickly
surrendering in peace and protecting your marriage in
worship. God is your rock and your fortress. There is no

greater love than the love of God. Understanding God's worth will help you trust Him in every area of your life.

The lack of finances, jobs or sickness can pull your marriage together or tear it apart. Make the choice to worship and win no matter what. Couples that worship together grow together. Let your worship begin at home. Worship God together in prayer, praise and by reading His word. Think on His goodness, and rejoice. Sing songs of praise and become undignified in your worship as you remember all the endless reasons to praise and worship God.

If you and your spouse don't worship together, pray and ask God to grace you with the wisdom to know how. You may be at the place in your life where you are weeping in worship, waiting on your change. Don't faint. In the beginning years of our marriage we didn't worship together. God turned both of our hearts toward him through fasting and much prayer. Now we preach to one another as we write sermons, we dance in the spirit, we sing our favorite worship song together and we pray together. Our worship is for real and we have seen God move in our intimate midnight worship!

Intentionally Declare

I declare and decree that I will willfully worship God with my spouse daily and take authority over the enemy in the Name of Jesus. I will put God first in my marriage and my relationship with my spouse.

Declare:

_____

_____

_____

_____

_____

Does your worship please God? Do you and your spouse worship together?

*******DAILY INTENT*******

Intentionally ask your spouse to sing your favorite worship song. Don't be angry if they don't know it.   Share with your spouse why it is important for the two of you to worship God together. Commit to set aside time to worship together daily.

_____

_____

_____

Outcome:

_____

_____

_____

Intentional Tools

Let everything that hath breath praise the LORD. Praise ye the LORD.

Psalms 150:6

O come, let us sing unto the LORD: let us make a joyful noise to the rock of our salvation.

Psalms 95:1

But the hour cometh, and now is, when the true worshippers shall worship the Father in spirit and in truth: for the Father seeketh such to worship him.

John 4:23

By him therefore let us offer the sacrifice of praise to God continually, that is, the fruit of our lips giving thanks to his name.

Hebrews 13:15

His Initials   Date   Her Initials   Date

Commit to Daily Prayer

Use today's topic and write a prayer for your spouse.
Earnestly commit to pray for them daily.

_____

_____

_____

_____

_____

Day 8

Intentionally Encourage

Wherefore comfort yourselves together, and edify one another, even as also ye do. I Thessalonians 5:11

The bible encourages us as Christians and we must encourage one another. Be the first one to speak life over your spouse daily. Even before the children or the co-workers can share great words of encouragement, greet one another with tenderness and a kiss. Pray about what to say, your facial expression and even your body language. If you are not having a great day, share your heart. Be honest and let your spouse know that you need their prayers today. Understand that the lack of encouragement teeters on rejection. It is easy for a spouse to feel rejected from you, when everyone else that crosses their path tells them how wonderful they are, yet they never hear it from you, from who it matters the most.

Healthy communication between spouses increases self worth with one another and builds trust. Some days we need more encouragement than the day before and it helps when your spouse knows just what to say. After a difficult day at work, maybe you didn't get the job you interviewed for or maybe you lost your job. Just know that whenever you encourage your spouse during a failure, those words reach deeper than an hour of praise after great success.

Maybe you have failed in the past at encouraging your spouse to reach for their dreams or desires. Allow this lesson to help you to work through your struggle. Perhaps your wife needs to be encouraged to keep doing a great job with the children. Your husband may feel his heart leap an extra beat just to hear you compliment him on how well he cares for your car. If you are unsure of what to say or how to say it ask your spouse, not your friend, what is most important to them. Listen to them and practice encouraging them when you are alone. Use every open opportunity to encourage your spouse. Watch their body language for signs that you got it right this time and made a home run.

Look to God together and know that He gave His word to encourage us all. Love on one another daily and "Stay Encouraged!"

Intentionally Declare

I declare and decree that moving forward we will speak life over our marriage in the Name of Jesus. I will put God first in my marriage and my relationship with my spouse.

Declare:

_____

_____

_____

_____

_____

How often do you encourage your spouse?

####### *******DAILY INTENT*******

Intentionally write down five ways that you can encourage your spouse. Practice them and then try them with your spouse.

Next, pray for God's will in your marriage and look for new ways to encourage your spouse.

1._____

2._____

3._____

4._____

5._____

Outcome:

_____

_____

_____

Intentional Tools

Arise, shine; for thy light is come, and the glory of the Lord
is risen upon thee.
Isaiah 60:1

But none of these things move me, neither count I my life
dear unto myself, so that I might finish my course with joy,
and the ministry, which I have received of the Lord Jesus,
to testify the gospel of the grace of God.

Luke 12:6 & 7

Let not mercy and truth forsake thee: bind them about thy
neck; write them upon the table of thine heart: So shalt thou
find favour and good understanding in the sight of God and
man.
Proverbs 3:3 & 4

Now therefore, if ye will obey my voice indeed, and keep

my covenant, then ye shall be a peculiar treasure unto me

above all people: for all the earth is mine.

Exodus 19:5

His Initials   Date   Her Initials   Date

Commit to Daily Prayer

Use today's topic and write a prayer for your spouse.
Earnestly commit to pray for them daily.

_____

_____

_____

_____

_____

Day 9

Intentionally Kind

And be ye kind one to another, tenderhearted, forgiving one another, even as God for Christ's sake hath forgiven you. Ephesians 4:32

The act of being kind and forgiving is a decision. Kindness must be practiced daily to remain mindful and considerate of your spouse throughout your relationship. The kinder path teaches us not to throw darts but to use thought in sharing dislike for actions that cause pain. When we learn how to be kind, we realize the importance of kindness whether we are happy or angry. The expression of anger doesn't mean that you are being unkind. Although, choosing not to be kind is doubly hurtful and usually escalates the issues quicker. The outcome disrupts your peace, your growth and your intimacy. It is easier to be kind when you are well rested and life shares its smile. Kindness is often a little more difficult after a hard day or a disagreement. When either of you are tired, small problems look bigger, offenses come easier, your focus is on short term decisions instead of what will be best in the long term. Your expression of kindness even when you are angry reveals your level of maturity. Remember kindness helps you to be heard and not just seen.

It takes practice and wisdom to express kind behavior consistently, especially when you are unhappy. Here are several powerful ways that you can cultivate a habit of kindness in your relationship daily. Each of these ways will produce peace, growth and intimacy. Try these daily and chart your consistency.

1. Accept responsibility for your actions, be honest.

2. Calmly share your thoughts without rage or daggers.

3. Tell your spouse something you appreciate about them often.

4. Hide a love note in your spouse's car or wallet.

5. Text or e-mail your spouse throughout the day.

6. Assist your spouse with one of their chores, lighten the load.

Over the years, we have learned how to speak kindly one to another. We have also learned that there are times when we should not even speak at all. Sometimes the kindness in our silence speaks louder than anything that we could think or imagine to say.

Intentionally Declare

I declare and decree that words of kindness will flow like rivers of living water to my spouse to build up our relationship in the Name of Jesus. I will put God first in my marriage and my relationship with my spouse.

Declare:

_____

_____

_____

_____

_____

Would your spouse say that you are genuinely kind?

*******DAILY INTENT*******

Intentionally write down four ways that you will show kindness to your spouse. Practice them daily and chart your consistency, not your spouses response.

Next, pray for God's will in your marriage and look for new ways to be kind to your spouse.

1._____
2._____
3._____
4._____

Outcome:

_____

_____

_____

Intentional Tools

She opened her mouth with wisdom and in her tongue is
the law of kindness.

Proverbs 31:26

Put on therefore, as the elect of God, holy and beloved,
bowels of mercies, kindness, humbleness of mind,
meekness, longsuffering.

Colossians 3:12

Charity suffers long and is kind; charity envy's not; charity
vaunted not itself, is not puffed up; doth not behave itself
unseemly, seeks not her own, is not easily provoked, thinks
no evil; rejoices not in iniquity, but rejoices in the truth;
bears all things, believes all things, hopes all things,
endures all things.

I Corinthians 13:4 - 7

His Initials   Date   Her Initials   Date

Commit to Daily Prayer

Use today's topic and write a prayer for your spouse.
Earnestly commit to pray for them daily.

_____

_____

_____

_____

_____

Day 10

Intentionally Pray

Therefore, I say unto you, what things so ever you desire, when you pray, believe that you receive them and you shall have them. Mark 11:24

As our marriage has matured, we have learned that praying together works. We have struggled through many different issues and at times we felt like giving up. It was in those moments that God intervened and reminded us that together, WE could do all things as He strengthens us. Now we pray together daily for the move of God in our marriage, our home, with our children, our families, our jobs and all that is attached to us. We are committed to God in all things. Standing in agreement for what we need has allowed us to see God at work in our lives. Through prayer we learned to trust God to know our hearts and help us to honor Him and one another daily.

There is power in the unity of prayer. Couples that pray together are united spiritually and believe that they are stronger as one. As you take your prayer request to God as one, you reap the benefits of answered prayers and the witness of the word of God.

Every married couple should have the desire to surrender their "STUFF" to God and believe for better. The "STUFF" that has the potential to keep couples separated from God and one another. Rebuke the enemy in your marriage through prayer and anything else that will keep either of you from walking in unity. Take authority over your "STUFF" and trust God to heal you in every broken area. Trust Him to restore your marriage and set you free. Make the decision to be better. Make the decision that you want your marriage to work. Learn to walk in the power of prayer with a willing heart to gut out all the dead and dry places in your marriage through prayer. Pray together and release your "STUFF" like, infidelity, catastrophic illness, death, financial lack, alcoholism, depression, drug abuse, jealousy, rejection and /or abuse. Release these things to God for total deliverance. As you pray, keep in mind that healing takes on its own shape in your individual lives. God has the power to instantly heal each of you. Knowing this, you must remain focused throughout your healing process and patient realizing that you may not both heal in the same areas at the same time.

Intentionally Declare

I declare and decree that I will pray without ceasing over our relationship and cancel the assignment of the enemy over our marriage in the Name of Jesus. I will put God first in my marriage and my relationship with my spouse.

Declare:

_____

_____

_____

_____

_____

Each of you may accept your total healing at varying stages. Do you and your spouse pray together daily?

*******DAILY INTENT*******

Intentionally write down the five things that you and your spouse can go to God in prayer for together.

Commit to praying together daily and write down how God favors you with answers to your prayers.

1._____
2._____
3._____
4._____
5._____

Outcome:

_____

_____

_____

Intentional Tools

If two of you agree on earth concerning anything that they ask, it will be done for them...

Matthew 18:19

This is the confidence we have in approaching God: that if we ask anything according to His will, He will hear us.

I John 5:14

And if we know that He hears us, whatever we ask, we know that we have what we asked of Him.

I John 5:15

If my people who are called by my name will humble themselves and pray and seek my face and turn from their wicked way, then I will hear from heaven and I will forgive their sin and will heal their land.

II Chronicles 7:14

His Initials   Date   Her Initials   Date

Commit to Daily Prayer

Use today's topic and write a prayer for your spouse.
Earnestly commit to pray for them daily.

_____

_____

_____

_____

_____

Day 11

Intentionally Honest

Lie not one to another, seeing that ye have put off the old man with his deeds; and have put on the new man, which is renewed in knowledge after the image of Him that created Him. Colossians 3:9 & 10

The words I love you mean more when you know that they are spoken from a place of truth and not a lie. When your spouse tells you, I need you and I never want to be without you, you want to believe them and trust that they are being genuine and truthful.

Being honest isn't always easy, but trust is built in relationships when the voice of honesty is heard and believed. It is more difficult for some spouses to be honest than others, based on prior relationships and personal circumstances. Some spouses conceal their emotional hurt and pain by hiding their negative feelings inside. On the other hand, some get angry and instead of hiding their feelings, they say things that they don't mean just to hurt the other. These behaviors are damaging to any relationship and it fosters more lies and deception. When one lie is told, another lie is sure to follow with the intent to cover the next lie that will be told until it all explodes. Refuse to be dishonest, instead walk in integrity and truth.

Choose to be honest in your relationship, especially in difficult situations. Honesty escalates love and trust to a greater level and strengthens your relationship. Truthfully share how you feel about the things that are important to you in your marriage. Perhaps you feel that sometimes it is easier to avoid conflict and a lengthy conversation by simply saying, "I'm ok!" It is fine, not to always be ok. Just be honest. Maintain clear lines of communication and suggest having difficult conversations at a different time when it is easier to share. Remember, until you learn what is important to each other, you will continue to stumble when trying to say the right thing. Remain honest, do it afraid. Be truthful!

"If you want to be trusted, just be honest." *Kushandwizdom*
"Be honest, brutally honest. That is what's going to maintain relationship." *Lauryn Hill*
"If you tell the truth, you don't have to remember anything." *Mark Twain*

Intentionally Declare

I declare and decree every word that flows from my mouth
will be spoken with honest intent and compassion towards
my spouse in the Name of Jesus. I will put God first in my
marriage and my relationship with my spouse.

Declare:

_____

_____

_____

_____

_____

Do you have trouble being honest with your spouse about how you really feel?

*******DAILY INTENT*******

Intentionally write down three things that you need to honestly share with your spouse.

Commit to praying together daily and write down how God favors you with answers to your prayers.

1._____

2._____

3._____

Outcome:

_____

_____

_____

Intentional Tools

Lying lips are an abomination to the Lord: but they that deal truly are His delight.

Proverbs 12:22

And ye shall know the truth and the truth shall make you free.

John 8:32

Finally, brethren whatsoever things are true, whatsoever things are honest, whatsoever things are just, whatsoever things are pure, whatsoever things are lovely, whatsoever things are of good report; if there be any virtue and if there be any praise, think on these things.

Philippians 4:8-9

Lie not one to another, seeing that ye have put off the old man with his deeds.

Colossians 3:9

His Initials   Date   Her Initials   Date

Commit to Daily Prayer

Use today's topic and write a prayer for your spouse.
Earnestly commit to pray for them daily.

_____

_____

_____

_____

_____

Day 12

Intentionally Faithful

A faithful man shall abound with blessings: but he that makes haste to be rich shall not be innocent. Proverbs 28:20

When we married we professed our love and loyalty to one another. We vowed to be faithful in sickness and in health, whether richer or poorer and unto death do us part. We have put our heart into loving one another with Godly love and trusting God to be our strength. Over the years, we have seen many days filled with sunshine and we have had some days where we hoped for the sun to shine. Through it all, our love has grown stronger and our commitment to one another has been unfailing. We learned to be faithful by spending time together daily. We vowed not to put others ahead of each other. We shared our needs and wants and worked on how to accomplish them the best way. As we shared earlier, there were a lot of days filled with sunshine. Equally, there were many days that we wondered how long this learning process would be and if we would part before death or not. We survived and so can you, but you must put in the work. Being faithful and remaining faithful to building one another up is a lifelong commitment that must be lived out until death.

Faithfulness is built on trust. Build your relationship by getting to know what makes your spouse unique. Remove the room for suspicion and doubt. Ask questions, be observant, give God your insecurities and be quick to forgive, especially the things that you don't understand. Don't allow the enemy to use your mind to create open doors that don't deserve your time or energy. When you and your spouse face the challenge of disagreement or accusations of betrayal, immediately stop and acknowledge how you both feel. Do everything in your power to remove all insecurities and maintain your faithfulness to one another. Agree to trust, but be honest and know when you have broken the vow of trust through unfaithful behavior. Be accountable for your actions and be mindful that you must work as a team. Nourish your intimacy in your marriage and let your spouse know that you are committed to their happiness. Learn to live, laugh and love with each other. Pray together, be honest, committed and faithful. Don't cheat, lie or steal the joy and happiness that your marriage could enjoy because you refuse to mature and grow up. Faithfully cherish and build the love you both deserve together!

Intentionally Declare

I declare and decree that the spirit of infidelity is destroyed in my marriage and replaced with true commitment only to my spouse in the Name of Jesus. I will put God first in my marriage and my relationship with my spouse.

Declare:

_____

_____

_____

_____

_____

_____

In what area have you caused your spouse not to trust you due to unfaithfulness?

*******DAILY INTENT*******

Intentionally write down four ways you could be more faithful to your spouse.

Commit to praying together daily and write down how God favors you with answers to your prayers.

1._____

2._____

3._____

4._____

Outcome:

_____

_____

_____

Intentional Tools

He that is faithful in that which is least is faithful also in much…

Luke 16:10

Moreover, it is required in stewards that a man be found faithful.

I Corinthians 4:2

Let not mercy and truth forsake thee: bind them about thy neck; write them upon the table of thine heart: So shalt thou find favor and good understanding in the sight of God and man.

Proverbs 3:3 – 4

Nevertheless, my lovingkindness will I not utterly take from him, nor suffer my faithfulness to fail.

Psalms 89:33

His Initials   Date   Her Initials   Date

Commit to Daily Prayer

Use today's topic and write a prayer for your spouse.
Earnestly commit to pray for them daily.

_____

_____

_____

_____

_____

Day 13

Intentionally Manipulative

That no man goes beyond and defraud his brother in any matter: because that the Lord is the avenger of all such, as we also have forewarned you and testified. I Thessalonians 4:5-6

Don't be manipulative. Every relationship deals with the rise and fall of emotions, some good and some bad. This sea of emotions is difficult in relationships when one spouse wants to control the other. Manipulation is a form of control. Creating drama is a typical way of getting one spouse to back down from what is important to them and the healthiness of the relationship, for selfish reasons.

Stop and think about how your relationship is setup. It's not very difficult to control someone that has been made to feel uncomfortable in their surroundings. Does everything revolve around your spouse and what they enjoy? Do you and your spouse live in each other's world or do you live in your spouse's world? Does your spouse consistently initiate situations that cause you to question if you are good enough for them? Do you walk gingerly around your spouse to know when it's best to speak or not speak? These are all measures of control and manipulation. Does your relationship suffer from these or other unhealthy manipulative and controlling tactics? If so, who is the manipulator? Maybe you are the manipulator in your relationship and you don't realize how your actions negatively affect your spouse. Perhaps your spouse has tried to share how uncomfortable this behavior is and you receive it as complaining.

Practice the five steps listed as you peacefully change the path or your relationship.

1. Access the situation.

2. Ask the hard questions.

3. Actively listen to the answers.

4. Accept responsibility for your actions.

5. Apologize and eliminate emotional turmoil.

Once the playing field has been leveled, you and your spouse can learn how to live in each other's world. Next, intentionally replace manipulation with appreciation.

Intentionally Declare

I declare and decree that every demonic weapon is cancelled that has been released over my marriage and my family in the Name of Jesus. I will put God first in my marriage and my relationship with my spouse.

Declare:

_____

_____

_____

_____

_____

Does your relationship suffer from manipulation or control issues?

Intentionally write down four areas of control that you are willing to accept as negative behavior in your relationship and eliminate them without anger.

Commit to praying together daily and write down how God strengthens you to release these areas of control and more.

1._____

2._____

3._____

4._____

Outcome:

_____

_____

_____

Intentional Tools

And Jesus answered and said unto them, take heed that no man deceives you.

Matthew 24:4

Now the works of the flesh are manifest, which are these, adultery, fornication, uncleanness, lasciviousness, idolatry, witchcraft, hatred, variance, emulations, wrath, strife, seditions, heresies, envying's, murders, drunkenness, revelling's and such like: of the which I tell you before, as I have also told you in time past, that they which do such things shall not inherit the kingdom of God.

Galatians 5:19 - 21

For we wrestle not against flesh and blood but against principalities against powers, against the rulers of the darkness of this world, against spiritual wickedness in high place.

His Initials   Date   Her Initials   Date

Commit to Daily Prayer

Use today's topic and write a prayer for your spouse.
Earnestly commit to pray for them daily.

_____

_____

_____

_____

_____

Day 14

Intentionally Intimate

For this reason, a man will leave his father and mother and be united to his wife, and they will become one flesh. Genesis 2:24

Intimacy with your spouse should be a pleasure. Each spouse should take the time to learn how to intimately minister to the other. In almost every relationship, one spouse desires the pleasure of sexual intimacy more often than the other. As a result, one spouse could have sex more often than desired or one spouse could have sex less than desired. This difference in desire is sometimes as a result of libido issues, better known as your sex drive. Other reasons for the difference in desire and frequency can be daily fatigue, marital issues, physical health, negative self-image, previous sexual abuse and/or children.

Share with your spouse your desire to be intimate with them and agree on the pace that will keep you both totally engaged every time. Talk to one another and avoid taking the other for granted. Don't allow your intimate memories from your past to crossover into your marriage and breed tension, comparison or disrespect. Discuss style, sensitivity to touch, past abusive issues, the need for foreplay, things that cause frustration, and great pleasure. Be adults and always respect one another in love and intimacy.

Divorce proof your marriage by choosing to stay committed to one another. Pray and stay away from tempting situations that will compromise your unity. Guard your eyes and ears from pornography and all sexual immorality. As the husband, learn to love your wife as Christ loved the church and fulfil your marital duty wholeheartedly to your wife. Be the Godly man that will love, honor and cherish her to the best of your ability. Likewise, wives serve your husbands with gladness, remembering that just as the husband's body belongs to you, your body belongs to him.

Enjoy the time you spend in intimacy with your spouse. Create times to laugh and play with each other. Seek ways to remove the daily stress of life by complimenting each other frequently. Don't be selfish! Intentionally ensure that both of you are satisfied and being served.

Intentionally Declare

I declare and decree that I will not lust after or desire the love or passion for anyone other than my spouse in the Name of Jesus. I will put God first in my marriage and my relationship with my spouse.

Declare:

_____

_____

_____

_____

_____

Throughout your day, do you think of intimate times that you and your spouse have enjoyed?

*******DAILY INTENT*******

Intentionally plan an intimate evening with your spouse. Surprise them with the things that you know will put a smile on their face and yours too.

_____

_____

_____

Outcome:

_____

_____

_____

Intentional Tools

Thou hast ravished my heart, my sister, my spouse; thou hast ravished my heart with one of thine eyes, with one chain of thy neck. How fair is thy love, my sister, my spouse! How much better is thy love than wine! And the smell of thine ointments than all spices!

Song of Solomon 4:9 & 10

Marriage is honorable in all, and the bed undefiled: but whoremongers and adulterers God will judge.

Hebrews 13:4

Flee fornication. Every sin that a man doeth is without the body; but he that committeth fornication sinneth against his own body.

I Corinthians 6:18

His Initials   Date   Her Initials   Date

Commit to Daily Prayer

Use today's topic and write a prayer for your spouse.
Earnestly commit to pray for them daily.

_____

_____

_____

_____

_____

Day 15

Intentionally Compliment

A virtuous woman is a crown to her husband: but she that makes ashamed is as rottenness in his bones. Proverbs 12:4

I can't think of a couple who doesn't like to hear kind words of encouragement and wear the smile that accompanies the sound of a compliment. Compliments feel great to everyone, and for some it doesn't matter whether they are giving the compliment or receiving it. Words have a way of tearing us down sometimes but when intentionally used for good, words can and will build us up. Share the words with your spouse that add life. Help maintain your spouse's self-worth by being their biggest fan and focus on what's good and not always what is not so good. Find joy in restoring peace in the lives of others. Be consistent in letting your spouse know that you appreciate them. Compliment them on how beautiful or handsome they are, how amazing they look in their outfit and even how attracted you are to them. Look into the eyes of your spouse often and genuinely compliment them. Men often need to hear their wives tell them that they are a great provider, a wonderful father, that the wife is proud of him and that he is handsome and still makes her smile. Women love to hear kind words from their man also. A great way to see her smile, is by kissing her good bye in the morning and simply saying, you make me happy or I love you and I can't wait to get back home to you.

Sometimes even though we have great intentions to say and do the right thing, the words just don't come out right. Perhaps you did not have a great example of someone who shared the importance of complimenting others. Guard your words and avoid the negative statements that are often painful and steal your spouse's peace. Focus on the positive things in your relationship instead of the negative. Don't take your spouse for granted. Notice the things that he or she does well, such as their daily patterns and give kind expressions that even you would like to hear. If you are unsure, ask your spouse what makes them happy and help them to enjoy this happiness daily. Listen to your spouse and be quick to acknowledge the things that are important to them. Also apologize without hesitation, when you see or are told that you have hurt your spouse. Watch your body language and ensure that it is consistent with the words that you use to show love to your spouse. Compliment your spouse daily and watch your relationship grow stronger.

Intentionally Declare

I declare and decree that I will not have wondering eyes for another and that I will intentionally compliment my spouse daily in the Name of Jesus. I will put God first in my marriage and my relationship with my spouse.

Declare:

_____

_____

_____

_____

_____

_____

Throughout your day, do you think of intimate times that you and your spouse have enjoyed?

*******DAILY INTENT*******

Intentionally plan an intimate evening with your spouse. Surprise them with the things that you know will put a smile on their face and yours too.

_____

_____

_____

Outcome:

_____

_____

_____

Intentional Tools

Thou hast ravished my heart, my sister, my spouse; thou hast ravished my heart with one of thine eyes, with one chain of thy neck. How fair is thy love, my sister, my spouse! How much better is thy love than wine! And the smell of thine ointments than all spices!

Song of Solomon 4:9 & 10

Marriage is honorable in all, and the bed undefiled: but whoremongers and adulterers God will judge.

Hebrews 13:4

Flee fornication. Every sin that a man doeth is without the body; but he that committeth fornication sinneth against his own body.

I Corinthians 6:18

His Initials   Date   Her Initials   Date

Commit to Daily Prayer

Use today's topic and write a prayer for your spouse.
Earnestly commit to pray for them daily.

_____

_____

_____

_____

_____

Day 16

Intentionally Apologize

Confess your faults one to another, and pray one for another, that ye may be healed. The effectual fervent prayer of a righteous man availeth much.   James 5:16

Apologizing is necessary but not easy for everyone to do.   Sometimes after a disagreement neither you nor your spouse feels totally responsible for what has happened, and neither of you want to apologize. You are experiencing a sea of emotions and your peace is broken. One of you must be the bigger person and apologize to restore your unity.

Many thoughts keep us from quickly asking our spouse to forgive us. It is easy to think about what if's, such as, what if you take this major leap and apologize and your spouse refuses to forgive you? What if you are the one who always apologizes first? What if you apologize hoping that your spouse will do the same and they simply say ok to your apology, because they feel like you were the one who should apologize and not them? On the other hand, what if your spouse is grateful for your apology and shows love to you like never before? The latter is the hoped for response that heals and restores your passion.

Initially, we had two different ideas about the need to apologize. We had to learn that without understanding each other's perspective there were a lot of hurt feelings and unchecked emotions. We spent a lot of time feeling like we were each other's enemy and holding on to unnecessary pain because we hadn't learned how to work through it. We had to consistently remind ourselves that no matter how we felt about our disagreements, that we truly loved each other, and that our love outweighed the issue.

Whether your spouse accepts your apology or not, intentionally apologize. With a true apology, it requires a great deal of vulnerability and exposure of yourself to your spouse. Make every attempt to look into the eyes of your spouse and have a real heartfelt moment and say I'm sorry for _____. Constantly remind each other that your disagreement should not define your relationship. Recognize that your love for one another is far more important than the disagreement. Apologize and forgive your spouse so that you both can move on to greater things together.

Intentionally Declare

I declare and decree that I will be quick to apologize to my spouse and break every wicked pattern and cycle of pride in the Name of Jesus. I will put God first in my marriage and my relationship with my spouse.

Declare:

_____

_____

_____

_____

_____

Are you the spouse that finds it hard to apologize?

Intentionally practice apologizing to your spouse. Ask your spouse to tell you three things that you do that irritates them.

Use these simple steps to help you get better at apologizing:

1. Quickly express remorse and say I'm sorry or I apologize.
2. Acknowledge what you have done and take responsibility for the action.
3. Promise that you will work hard not to do the same thing again.
4. Watch your spouse's body language and ensure that you are believable.

Outcome:

_____

_____

_____

Intentional Tools

And be ye kind one to another, tenderhearted, forgiving one another, even as God for Christ's sake hath forgiven you.

Ephesians 4:32

And forgive us our sins; for we also forgive every one that is indebted to us. And lead us not into temptation; but deliver us from evil.

Luke 11:4

Likewise, ye younger, submit yourselves unto the elder. Yea, all [of you] be subject one to another, and be clothed with humility: for God resisteth the proud, and giveth grace to the humble.

I Peter 5:5

His Initials   Date   Her Initials   Date

Commit to Daily Prayer

Use today's topic and write a prayer for your spouse.

Earnestly commit to pray for them daily.

_____

_____

_____

_____

_____

Day 17
Intentionally Fireproof

The tongue has the power of life and death, and those who love it will eat its fruit. Proverbs 18:21

Our words have so much power. The lack of ineffective communication immediately takes the fire of love from our marriage and replaces it with the fire of rage. It doesn't matter what season your marriage is in today, you must fireproof your relationship for your tomorrow.

Each season demonstrates a period of endurance. Don't short circuit your joy by trading your intimacy for marital tension because you are not mature enough to weather your current storm. With tension, in any consistent wave, this opens the door for infidelity, separation or even divorce. Be careful to focus on your marriage as a whole and not on yourself and how the tension is making you feel. When all of the focus is individualized the marriage falls into a dying state because the life is being choked out of one half.

Choose a stance together and hold each other accountable for the good of the marriage. Minimize the urge to defend yourself by using more "I" statements and less "You" statements. Practice restating your desires for a safer delivery and better outcome. Share your desire by saying, "I" am feeling overwhelmed at work and "I" need more help caring for the children. This verbiage would replace a more confrontational statement, such as, "You" are not helping me enough with caring for the children and it's too much for me right now. If you have not asked for help, don't assume that your spouse will notice that your stress level has increased and that perhaps you could use a little more help.

Be open and transparent and effectively communicate. Acknowledge the good that your spouse has done and find positive ways to constructively express the change you hope to see. Your marriage will survive based on the position you take and how you manage your emotions. Look to the Lord for guidance. Learn to speak each other's language, even in silence. One of you may communicate through silence and the other may communicate through touch. Focus on what works and work that format. Be intentional in your conversations. Handle conflict respectfully. Use your power to avoid negative silent treatment, avoid screaming and yelling, avoid hitting or shoving and avoid sharing your private business with the wrong people.

Fireproof your marriage by surviving together through open and honest communication, forgiveness and oneness. Walk in faith and not fear that your love will produce the fire that makes relationships fun and lasting. Share your deepest secrets, accept failures, embrace physical changes, and always tell each other the truth. Positive communication will always prove to be fruitful.

Greg is an actor and early in our marriage he was offered several opportunities to travel doing stage plays. At the time, we had already started our family. Greg made the decision to only perform in the plays that were local and not the plays that would take him from home for long periods of time. He made the decision that he believed was best for our family, with hopes that God would still open doors for him. Over the years, God opened doors in theater and films like, Mama Flora's Family, Eddie, The Epidemic, Pay the Price and Birth of a Nation to name a few. I can't imagine how a reverse decision would have affected our love and our relationship. I believe that his decision helped to fireproof our relationship in its young and infant stage, so that we could enjoy happiness and wholeness today.

Intentionally Declare

I declare and decree that I will avoid all ungodly distractions as we press forward according to the Word of God in the Name of Jesus. I will put God first in my marriage and my relationship with my spouse.

Declare:

_____

_____

_____

_____

_____

Before you go to bed tonight leave a love note in the windshield of your spouse's car.

*******DAILY INTENT*******

Intentionally take steps to fireproof your relationship by choosing not to say anything negative to your spouse today. Surprise your spouse by doing something special and unexpected that you know they would appreciate. Use this space to write out your plan.

_____

_____

_____

Outcome:

_____

_____

_____

Intentional Tools

A virtuous woman is a crown to her husband: But she that maketh ashamed is as rottenness in his bones.

Proverbs 12:4

Whoso findeth a wife findeth a good thing, And obtaineth favour of the LORD.

Proverbs 18:22

House and riches are the inheritance of fathers: And a prudent wife is from the LORD.

Proverbs 19:14

Most men will proclaim everyone his own goodness: But a faithful man who can find? The just man walketh in his integrity: His children are blessed after him

Proverbs 20:6-7

Who can find a virtuous woman? For her price is far above rubies.

Proverbs 31:10

His Initials   Date   Her Initials   Date

Commit to Daily Prayer

Use today's topic and write a prayer for your spouse.
Earnestly commit to pray for them daily.

_____

_____

_____

_____

_____

Day 18

Intentionally Unselfish

Look not every man on his own things, but every man also on the things of others. Philippians 2:4

There are multiple scriptures relevant to a man leaving his father and mother and being joined to his wife, and the two becoming one flesh. However, I am partial to Ephesians, because it says "it is a great mystery!" One of the keys to unlocking the marital mystery is being unselfish. You have to perfect the art of being interested in, being generous to and being concerned about the welfare of your spouse. The union of a man and woman in holy matrimony is the beginning of the road to true unselfishness if you desire a marriage that works!

Adam and Eve were the first and only couple that entered into a covenant relationship that shared DNA! Every martial relationship after it had to achieve oneness without that bond. This reason is why becoming one is so challenging. You have lived your entire life into adulthood and only had to be concerned about the welfare of people that shared the same DNA with you. Because you have the same DNA, your likes, dislikes and quirks will more than likely be similar in nature and if not tolerable, at least understandable. However, when two people make a decision to become one flesh, it requires another level of unselfishness. Now you have to create a covenant bond with someone who you think you know something about, but in reality you don't know where ANY of the skeletons of their life are buried. One of our friends put it this way, when you say I do, you sign a death certificate to who you were as a single man and YOU are the executioner. The death can be quick and painless much like lethal injection, firing squad or electrocution. Or, it can be slow and painful, much like death from 1,000,000 paper cuts! And it all depends on how unselfish you are.

Becoming one flesh was a mystery to me because I only looked at it from a literal prospective and it never made sense to me. But when I matured a little more and started to understand the concept from a figurative place it began to come together for me. When you and your spouse first get married you start to see her likes, dislikes and differences. Over time you develop a pattern of doing the things that will elicit positive responses and you release the things that conjure up negative responses. As you perfect those behaviors, the single man and woman you were dies, and the new married couple starts to emerge. As this change occurs, we can better understand the term "two becoming one flesh."

Only God knows if your marriage will ever achieve utopia. Marriage is one of the hardest job of your life. In this job, you never get a day off, you can't take sick days or a vacation from the union, yet it can be one of the most rewarding experiences of your life. Remember you don't get it right until you become so unselfish that your spouse's needs, wants and desires become your needs, wants and desire. Then you can close the casket on the brother you were at the altar and be resurrected as "one."

Intentionally Declare

I declare and decree that I will be considerate of my spouse and create a safe environment daily in the Name of Jesus. I will put God first in my marriage and my relationship with my spouse.

Declare:

_____

_____

_____

_____

_____

Has your spouse ever told you that you are selfish? Is it true?

Intentionally think of something that you know you are unwilling to share with your spouse. Ask your spouse to name some things that you selfishly do that irritates them. Try not to get angry as they share. Use this space to write these things down and commit to change this behavior.

_____

_____

_____

Outcome:

_____

_____

_____

Intentional Tools

Be kindly affectionate one to another with brotherly love; in honor preferring one another. **Romans 12:10**

We then that are strong ought to bear the infirmities of the weak, and not to please ourselves. Let every one of us please his neighbor for his good to edification. For even Christ pleased not himself; but, as it is written, the reproaches of them that reproached thee fell on me.

Romans 15:1-3

Let no man seek his own, but every man another's wealth.

I Corinthians 10:24

Even as I please all men in all things, not seeking mine own profit, but the profit of many, that they may be saved.

I Corinthians 10:33

His Initials   Date   Her Initials   Date

Commit to Daily Prayer

Use today's topic and write a prayer for your spouse.
Earnestly commit to pray for them daily.

_____

_____

_____

_____

_____

Day 19

Intentionally Non-Abusive

Envy, murders, drunkenness, revelries, and the like; of which I tell you beforehand, just as I also told *you* in time past, that those who practice such things will not inherit the kingdom of God. But the fruit of the Spirit is love, joy, peace, longsuffering, kindness, goodness, faithfulness, gentleness, self-control. Against such there is no law. Galatians 5:21-22

Two things generally occur when you see negative experiences as a child. You grow up to repeat the behavior, or you act in an equal and opposite manner of the negative behavior you witnessed. Either way the visual picture leaves an indelible imprint in your brain that you have to deal with, so that this negative experience doesn't deal with you. As a kid I witnessed domestic violence and it was not something that I think that any kid should witness or have to deal with. I tried to block it out when I saw it and thought that I forgot about it until I became an adult and got married.

Every marriage experiences rough patches and Shonda and I are no different. I am not proud to say that during some of our rough patches, there were times that I resorted to verbal abuse. I am a firm believer that with God all things are possible and forgiveness is available for all things. I am grateful that we never experienced any physical abuse like I witnessed as a child. First of all, a physically abusive spousal episode is something that in my sight would be extremely difficult to overcome. Even on my worst day when I'm as hot as fish grease with Shonda, I could never intentionally do something to physically harm or damage her, she is MY rib! Secondly, I don't believe I married the type of women that would easily forgive an action like that and would probably retaliate physically and rightfully so. Finally, I just don't thing I could forgive myself.

Here are some practical tools to avoid falling prey to abusive behavior; do everything humanly possible to stay at peace with everyone, including your spouse. Disagreements will inevitably come up, but love covers a multitude of sins. Practice the fruits of the spirit; love, joy, peace, longsuffering, kindness, goodness, faithfulness, gentleness, self-control. Be brutally honest with yourself. If you have those urges or impulses that are bent towards abusive behavior, seek professional help. Lastly, get to know Jesus in an intimate way because becoming His disciple can help you treat your spouse like the God vessel that she is.

Refrain from insulting your spouse, or speaking harshly to him or her. Learn to love your spouse as yourself and put away all childish behavior and thought processes. Don't abuse the gift that God has so graciously given to you. The scripture notes, "Whoso findeth a wife, findeth a good thing, and obtaineth favor of the Lord," Proverbs 18:22. Love your good gift without abusing it and, "Let no corrupt communication proceed out of your mouth, but that which is good to the use of edifying, that it may minister grace unto the hearers." Ephesians 4:29

Intentionally Declare

I declare and decree that I will protect my spouse and not allow the enemy to rule my tongue or my attitude in the Name of Jesus. I will put God first in my marriage and my relationship with my spouse.

Declare:

_____

_____

_____

_____

_____

Seek God for help to eliminate all poisonous behavior that inflicts abuse on your spouse.

*******DAILY INTENT*******

Intentionally think of the unhealthy and abusive behavior that you may have witnessed in your past. Ask your spouse if you have given them any reason to feel afraid of them or unsafe.

List any response that your spouse shares and together write a plan to correct this negative behavior.

_____

_____

_____

Outcome:

_____

_____

_____

Intentional Tools

Casting all your care upon Him; for He careth for you.

I Peter 5:7

The Lord is not slack concerning his promise, as some men count slackness; but is longsuffering to us-ward, not willing that any should perish, but that all should come to repentance.

II Peter 3:9

Let this mind be in you, which was also in Christ Jesus.

Philippians 2:5

And whatsoever ye shall ask in my name, that will I do, that the Father may be glorified in the Son.

John 14:13

His Initials   Date   Her Initials   Date

Commit to Daily Prayer

Use today's topic and write a prayer for your spouse.
Earnestly commit to pray for them daily.

Day 20

Intentionally Romantic

Draw me, we will run after thee: the king hath brought me into his chambers: we will be glad and rejoice in thee, we will remember thy love more than wine: the upright love thee. Song of Solomon 1:4

Being romantic, is the action related to the nature of romance. When you are in sync with your spouse it can be the most euphoric feeling in the world.

Here's what I've learned in 30 years of marriage; if you do your research on your spouse in three areas it will guarantee the romantic results you desire every time. Find out what your spouse loves sexually, mentally and physically and become a PHD in those areas. First, engage in some open and frank discussions about what your spouse loves sexually. Don't only talk about what your spouse loves, but have fun practicing and getting it right. Find out what turns your spouse on and become the expert on fulfilling that need. This will be a continuous procedure because as time goes on your spouses' needs will change due to child-bearing, age, stress and physical health. Continue to stay focused on her needs and you will grow closer. I promise you will reap the benefits of becoming the expert of pleasure in this regard. Secondly learn what stimulates your spouse mentally and become proficient in those things. Become her go to person on things that interest her. Surprise your spouse every now and then with some knowledge of something that she has taken an interest in. Remember that your spouse would appreciate you taking an active interest in what she's doing and showing that you care. Support her life's dreams, goals and vision. Share with her that you want her to achieve her life's missions. Let her know that her dreams matter to you.

Make her laugh as much as possible because laughter is good for the soul and is good like medicine. One other tip, learn what your spouse's love language is because that's a key indicator of things you can do to make love to her mind.

Be in the best physical shape you can be not only for your well-being but also for your spouse. A woman feels good knowing the man that she loves can physically take care of her and a man is proud to be seen with their woman looking physically good. Romance is more than just actions geared towards a physical outcome but a goal for mental and emotional happiness also.

Intentionally Declare

I declare and decree that I will be united with my spouse in true love and the power of Christ in the Name of Jesus. I will put God first in my marriage and my relationship with my spouse.

Declare:

_____

_____

_____

_____

_____

Do you enjoy being romantic with your spouse?

*******DAILY INTENT*******

Intentionally ask your spouse if they still desire the same romantic things that they did when you first got married. Take notes and work together to show your spouse that their romantic desires are important to you. Commit to do something new daily for the next 5 days.

_____

_____

_____

Outcome:

_____

_____

_____

Intentional Tools

Draw me after you and let us run together! The king has brought me into his chambers" "We will rejoice in you and be glad; We will extol your love more than wine. Rightly do they love you.

Solomon 1:4

Let your fountain be blessed, and rejoice in the wife of your youth.

Proverbs 5:18

Two are better than one because they have a good return for their labor.

Ecclesiastes 4:9

A garden locked is my sister, my bride, A rock garden locked, a spring sealed up.

Song of Solomon 4:12

Many waters cannot quench love, Nor will rivers overflow it; If a man were to give all the riches of his house for love, It would be utterly despised.

Song of Solomon 8:7

His Initials   Date   Her Initials   Date

Commit to Daily Prayer

Use today's topic and write a prayer for your spouse.
Earnestly commit to pray for them daily.

_____

_____

_____

_____

_____

Day 21
Intentionally Transformed

And be not conformed to this world: but be ye transformed by the renewing of your mind that ye may prove what is that good, and acceptable, and perfect will of God. Romans 12:2

God instructs us NOT to conform to this world. We are taught to change through transformation and by the renewing of our mind. The way we think, the way we remember, even the way we look at situations and individuals must change to prove what is that good, acceptable, and perfect will of God. Naturally so, as a caterpillar begins to undergo its remarkable transformation, called metamorphosis, what was once viewed as a small egg, short, stubby and without wings, will soon develop wings and fly. Like the caterpillar, both the man and the woman must go through the painful stages of transformation. They must transform their lives to love unconditionally by renewing their minds. On this road of intentional transformation each couple will experience vulnerability in an unexplainable way. This journey will round some curvy roads, go up some mountains and through some valleys while facing some harsh realities that must be changed. Each couple will find that, marriage is a commitment beyond the knowledge of the human mind. Marriage requires the love of God and His divine wisdom. Be intentional! Die to who you are on purpose so that God can use you for His glory and your spouse can love and appreciate you.

Like most young couples, we entered marriage with many ideas that had been shaped by our own childhood experiences and mindsets. We tried to build our new life on top of what we perceived to be solid foundations. The only problem was that we were trying to build one life on two foundations. We were setting ourselves up for failure because without realizing it, we were dividing our household, simply because of old mindsets. We hoped that our conversations about how we wanted to live our lives would be enough to live a happy and wholesome life together, but that wasn't enough. Just as Romans 12:2 instructs us not to conform to this world we learned the hard way that each of us had some family traditions that we could not conform to and stay married to one another. Noticing and identifying the things about our marriage that weren't fruitful wasn't the problem. The hard decision was deciding which experiences to hold on to. Neither of us wanted to believe that how our parents had raised us wasn't good enough for our marriage. The harsh reality was, we had to intentionally identify old patterns and outdated structures that would only lead us to bitterness or divorce.

Our transformation came in devoting time to learning the will of God. To save our lives and our marriage, we needed to know how to renew our minds. We had to be willing to endure the pain together and lean on each other in both good and bad times. We held on to important seeds that were planted from our past, we grew from those short and stubby ways of thinking and removed everything that we could that kept us from soaring high on the wings of love. It became important to know that we would never prove or experience God's good, acceptable and perfect will until we renewed our mindset. We are yet being transformed, but we are enjoying the journey together and building on a solid foundation that is not divided. We are IT, Intentionally Transformed!

Intentionally Declare

I declare and decree that I will intentionally love my spouse with all of my heart and be faithful in the Name of Jesus. I will put God first in my marriage and my relationship with my spouse.

Declare:

_____

_____

_____

_____

_____

What steps are you willing to take to intentionally transform your marriage?

*******DAILY INTENT*******

Intentionally identify and write down old mindsets that have kept your marriage stagnant. Decide what you are willing to give up and what you are willing to do to intentionally transform your marriage.

_____

_____

_____

Outcome:

_____

_____

_____

Intentional Tools

Therefore, if any man be in Christ, he is a new creature: old things are passed away; behold, all things are become new.

II Corinthians 5:17

But we all, with open face beholding as in a glass the glory of the Lord, are changed into the same image from glory to glory, even as by the Spirit of the Lord.

II Corinthians 3:18

I am crucified with Christ: nevertheless I live; yet not I, but Christ liveth in me: and the life which I now live in the flesh I live by the faith of the Son of God, who loved me, and gave himself for me.

Galatians 2:20

His Initials   Date   Her Initials   Date

Commit to Daily Prayer

Use today's topic and write a prayer for your spouse.
Earnestly commit to pray for them daily.

_____

_____

_____

_____

_____

CONCLUSION

God created marriage as an awesome institution for men and women to engage one another in unity. Your union did not catch God by surprise. "For He knows the plans that He has for you, saith the Lord, thoughts of peace and not of evil to give you an expected end." Jeremiah 29:11

It is our hope and prayer that since you are reading the conclusion that perhaps you have relinquished your plans for the plans of Christ. From this point forward, use this fresh start to forgive and to walk intentionally into your destiny together for a better life. Live to love and meet one another's needs. The honeymoon is over and no matter how long you have been married, you must continue to grow as one in unity. Go forth and experience Intentional Love!

Prayer

Heavenly Father, we are grateful for your loving kindness towards us. Lord, thank you for the skills of communication and the wisdom to help other couples. It is our prayer God that you will use this book as a tool to bring peace in the heart of every relationship.

Many of the couples reading this book Lord have been hurt and are hurting one another. Reveal to them the importance of true love according to your word. Break and destroy the struggles that keep them bound and from the freedom of true love. Deliver them from every stronghold of bondage.

Lord enable the couples to repent and forgive without holding grudges against one another. Allow them to receive your healing and victory in their lives.

Allow them to serve you and one another with all of their hearts. Thank you Father for the freedom to intentionally love on purpose with a renewed mind. In

Jesus Name, Amen.

About the Authors

Elders Greg and Shonda Holmes, are natives of North Carolina. Their foundational training in ministry was developed under the leadership of Overseer C.S. Lattimore of Bible Way Church of the Living God.

They are both anointed and equipped to teach and preach the word of God. Weekly they are given the chance to serve and honor their call at their local church, Elizabeth Baptist Church of Conyers, GA. Dr. C.L. Oliver is the Senior Pastor and Rev. Darrell Hall is the Campus Pastor.

Elder Greg Holmes is a faithful husband, father and friend. He is also an established Actor and Author. Holmes is in the process of filming a new documentary.

Elder Shonda Holmes enjoys being a loving wife and a mother to her children. Holmes is a skilled Accountant, Counselor and Certified Life Coach. She is also the CEO & Founder of, "I am IT, Intentionally Transformed."

Together they have enjoyed Intimate Love for over 30 years.

For more information, visit iamithope.com.

Intentional Tools

Wives, submit yourselves unto your own husbands, as unto the Lord. **Ephesians 5:22-23**

Whoso findeth a wife findeth a good thing, and obtaineth favour of the LORD. **Proverbs 18:22**

Marriage is honourable in all, and the bed undefiled; but whoremongers and adulterers God will judge.

Hebrews 13:4

Therefore shall a man leave his father and his mother, and shall cleave unto his wife: and they shall be one flesh.
Genesis 2:24

Husbands, love your wives, even as Christ also loved the church, and gave himself for it. **Ephesians 5:25**

It is better to dwell in a corner of the housetop, than with a brawling woman in a wide house. **Proverbs 21:9**

And Adam knew Eve his wife; and she conceived, and bare Cain, and said, I have gotten a man from the LORD.
Genesis 4:1

Intentional Tools

Thou shalt not commit adultery. **Exodus 20:14**

For thou hast possessed my reins: thou hast covered me in my mother's womb. **Psalms 139:13**

Drink waters out of thine own cistern, and running waters out of thine own well. **Proverbs 5:15**

Let her be as the loving hind and pleasant roe; let her breasts satisfy thee at all times; and be thou ravished always with her love. **Proverbs 5:19**

Let him kiss me with the kisses of his mouth, for thy love is better than wine. **Song of Solomon 1:2**

How fair is thy love, my sister, my spouse! How much better is thy love than wine! And the smell of thine ointments than all spices! **Song of Solomon 4:10**

But I say unto you, That whosoever looketh on a woman to lust after her hath committed adultery with her already in his heart. **Matthew 5:28**

Intentional Notes

Intentional Notes